THE WORLD OF BUGS

The world is just heaving with little leggy things. You can see them anywhere, almost anytime – lurking, creeping, scuttling or whizzing. But it can sometimes be hard to know exactly what you saw. The pictures in this book will help you to recognise some of the bugs you might find.

Six-legged ones are insects. Insects include beetles, flies, butterflies & moths, grasshoppers, ants, wasps & bees. They also include a group properly called 'bugs', which is confusing.

Many insects, such as beetles, flies and butterflies, start out as grubs, maggots or caterpillars (larvae), which look very different from the adults. It is hard for an adult insect to grow because its crunchy shell is also its skeleton, so all its muscles are attached to this bag of bones. But some insects, such as bugs and grasshoppers, do manage to begin as small versions of adults. They need to cast off their old skeleton (moult) several times as they grow, just as we throw away clothes that have become too small, and make a new one that fits. This general problem is one of the main reasons why insects do not grow very big, but what they lack in size they more than make up in numbers!

Spiders are the only animals in this book that have eight legs. They are not insects. Spiders also begin as tiny versions of the adults, and frequently moult their old skin-skeleton. This does not prevent some spiders from growing as big as a person's hand!

BUGS FACTS:
There are more species of insects on planet Earth than any other form of life.

SPIDERS

Spiders are the only creatures in this book that are not insects. Even though some insects (such as silkworms) can spin silk, spider-silk is in a class of its own. It is so special that scientists have been trying to copy it for many years. Spiders use up to 4 different kinds to build their webs.

Web-spiders use their feet to detect vibrations from a fly caught in their designer trap. Although they have several eyes, they have terrible eyesight. But not all spiders use a web to catch food. Many species are active hunters which stalk and pounce on prey like cats and dogs do. These hunting spiders generally have two huge shiny eyes – and excellent eyesight!

A spider cannot chew, but it can bite! Its two hollow fangs first inject a fast-acting poison that paralyses its prey. It may wrap the helpless, living victim in a skein of silk to carry away and eat later, or it may inject digestive juices immediately and then suck out the liquidised soup. Yummy!

As the trapped insect struggles to free itself, the web's vibrations tell the spider that dinner is ready!

Zebra spider

Swamp spider

Orb-web spider

Wolf spider with eggs

Red-back

Striped crab spider

SPIDER FACTS:

There are over 30,000 species of spider in the world. Spiders recycle their webs: when rebuilding, or repairing damage, they eat the old silk as they go along.

The bright eyes of a wolf.

THE WORLD'S MOST DANGEROUS SPIDER?

The Sydney funnel-web spider is one of the most dangerous creatures in the world – its bite can be lethal to humans. The female can be particularly aggressive, especially if her funnel-shaped web is disturbed.

Where in the world?

The Sydney funnel-web spider is found in Western Australia

Spiders can tackle prey larger than themselves.

If it survives, this tiny spiderling will eventually grow into a giant like its parent (bottom right).

The female Black Widow probably causes more human casualties than any other spider. This is mainly because she likes to lay her eggs in cellars and dark corners - especially under the seats of outdoor toilets!

Pink-kneed Tarantula

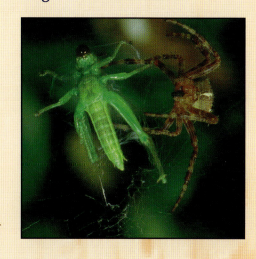

Flower spider
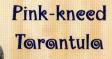

Close-up view of a spider's spinneret, or web-spinner, which can manufacture up to four varieties of silk.

BEETLES

Goliath Beetle

Beetles live nearly everywhere except in the oceans. Between them, they eat just about anything, including wood, bacon, and other animals' droppings.

Under their hard wing-cases (elytra), nearly all beetles have a pair of gauzy wings neatly packed away. Even water-beetles have wings, which is how they get to new ponds.

Larvae and adults of ladybird beetles feed on aphids (greenfly), longhorn beetles have larvae that feed on wood, dung beetles feed on (you guessed it!) dung, but atlas beetles do not eat atlases...

Like other adult insects, beetles breathe through a network of airpipes that run round their body. Even water-beetles need air; they come to the surface regularly to breathe out a bubble of stale air and take in a fresh supply - but you could be fooled if you didn't know that they breathe through their tail!

Longhorn

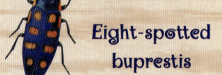
Carabid

Eight-spotted buprestis

Water beetles

Dung Beetle

BEETLE FACTS:

There are over 50,000 species of beetle in the world. The heaviest insect is a species of Goliath beetle that can weigh 3.5 ounces (100 grams).

Atlas beetle

THE WORLD'S MOST WANTED BEETLE

Before people began growing potatoes in the Rocky Mountains, the Colorado beetle lived there quietly on a diet of buffalo-bur leaves. It has now become a dreaded illegal immigrant wherever potatoes are grown.

Where in the world?
The Colorado beetle was first seen in Colorado, USA

In some parts of the world, shiny scarabs are worn as living jewels.

Longhorn

Splendid Buprestis

Cherry Chafer

Glow-worm larva (above) and adult female glow-worm (top) have no wings.

Atlas beetle

Close-up view of a female stag beetle's head and jaws

BUTTERFLIES

The pattern on a butterfly's wing is made of thousands of coloured scales. Those flashing wings are the end of a life-cycle that might have started, 2 years earlier, with an egg no bigger than a pinhead.

Butterflies begin as larvae called caterpillars. A caterpillar simply eats and eats until it has put on enough weight to make a butterfly. Then it finds a safe place to make its amazing transformation. Inside a hard shell (called a pupa or chrysalis), the caterpillar's body is totally reorganised. When it is ready, the pupa splits open and a butterfly emerges. Its brand-new wings are damp and crumpled. They need to be stretched and dried before it can fly away.

Adult butterflies only drink liquids. They usually suck sugary sap from flowers but some tropical butterflies sip soupy mud from puddles and riverbanks. Some butterflies only live long enough to mate and lay eggs, others hibernate through the winter and some (such as the Monarch) can migrate across oceans.

Swallowtail caterpillar

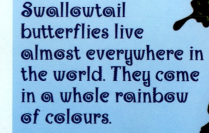

Monarch butterfly

Swallowtail butterflies live almost everywhere in the world. They come in a whole rainbow of colours.

BUTTERFLY FACTS:

Monarch butterflies can fly across the Atlantic. A caterpillar eats enough to increase its weight 1000 times between hatching and pupating.

THE WORLD'S LARGEST BUTTERFLY

Birdwings are swallowtails without tails. Their long front wings measure up to 10 inches across. This one is about 7 inches wide – just as wide as a person's head.

Where in the world? Birdwing butterflies live in the forests of Australasia.

Heliconius

Ruzmanova's swallowtail

Delias

Morpho

Owl butterfly

Sulphur

Close-up view of a Monarch butterfly's wing

PREDATORS

Ant Lion

Insects evolved before there were many other animals on dry land. This is why so many meat-eating insects eat other insects. And they have some fiendish tricks for trapping their neighbours!

Mantises lurk around looking just like part of the landscape, such as a leafy twig or even a flower, until some unsuspecting little fly or beetle comes within reach of those two lightning-sprung front legs. Once seized in their barbed grip, there is no escape.

Sharp-eyed robber-flies cruise around, hunting for other flying insects to clutch with their dangly, bristly legs. Then the robber sinks its sharp beak into its prey and sucks out the juices. Charming!

Backswimmer

Most of the 4,000 species of assassin bugs stick to stabbing other insects, but a small number – known as 'kissing bugs' – also bite people. The really bad news is that, as well as being very painful, their bite can carry some deadly tropical diseases.

The backswimmer is a water bug powerful enough to prey on small fish and frogs. Its beak is also strong enough to stab through human skin.

Among the weirdest predators are ant-lion larvae. These amazing creatures live at the bottom of a dry, sandy pit, waiting for an ant or other small insect to slide down the steep sides into their open jaws.

Assassin bug

Scorpion

MANTIS FACTS:
The female praying mantis eats her mate. Mantises are meat-eating cousins of grasshoppers and stick insects.

THE WORLD OF BUGS

DID YOU KNOW?

...that craneflies (also called daddy long legs) do all their eating as larvae called leatherjackets? The adults do not even have a mouth.

...that eyecatching colour combinations of yellow-and-black and red-and-black are used by many insects to show that they are poisonous or dangerous? Yellow and black striped wasps are dangerous. Red and black spotted ladybirds taste nasty.

...that the hairs from a caterpillar make your skin itch? They can also damage delicate parts of your eyes, so it makes sense not to touch them - no matter how silky-soft they look.

...that the males of some species of stick insects have never been seen? The females lay eggs (which all become females) without ever meeting a mate.

...that the 'manna' in the Bible is a sugary substance made by scale insects - relatives of greenflies - that live on tamarisk trees in Palestine?

...that giant waterbugs are a favourite food in parts of Asia?

...that there are more than four thousand species of ladybird beetles in the world?

...that it would take one thousand glow-worms to produce the same amount of light as an ordinary light-bulb.

...that some luminous click-beetles shine so brightly that only three or four of them give enough light to read by.

DID YOU KNOW?

…that there are more than 30 million different species of insects on planet Earth?

…that some wood-boring insects, such as sawflies, use a drill strengthened with metal?

…that the male Emperor moth can smell a female 11 km (6.8 miles) away?

…that the world's loudest insect, the male cicada, can be heard by a person 400m (.25 miles) away?

…that a stag beetle larva can squeak like a mouse? It may also take up to 7 years for the larva (feeding on rotting wood) to grow big enough to turn into a beetle 7 cm long

…that the larvae of lacewings flies are so bloodthirsty that lacewings lay their eggs separately, each at the end of a long stalk, to prevent the larvae eating one another as soon as they hatch?

…that a termite queen can lay more than 10 thousand eggs during the ten years of her life?

…that insects with wings existed more than 175 million years ago, at least 170 million years before the earliest human beings? Giant dragonflies from the Carboniferous age had a wingspan nearly 1 metre (3 feet) wide.

THE WORLD'S FIERCEST FEMALE

Female mantises are much bigger than the males. They are famous for their huge appetite, which is hardly ever satisfied even when their body is bloated with food. A female mantis normally eats her mate after mating. If she is really hungry, she may eat him even before the act of mating is finished!

Where in the world?
Mantises are found in most warm regions of the world.

A Mantis makes short work of this fly.

Mantis fly

Katydids resorting to cannibalism.

Close-up view of a mantis's head.

FLIES

The name 'fly' really means an insect with only one pair of wings. Strictly speaking, then, dragonflies and damselflies are not true flies. Another difference between real flies and dragonflies is the way they feed. True flies can only handle liquid food with their sucking tongue, but dragons and damsels have a weird mouth that shoots right off their face to snap up whole insects to eat.

But flies are not feeble. They can stab and spit as well as suck. Some flies can make a hole in another insect's armour, or the thick skin of a cow, to inject digestive enzymes and suck up the digested meat. Their larvae (maggots) normally burrow right inside their food, using spiny hooks around their mouth to help them. Depending on the species, the food that fly larvae dig into includes fruit, faeces, and even living flesh. Most fly larvae have no eyes or legs, because they do not need any.

Not all flies have totally horrible habits. Although their larvae are parasites of bees and other insects, beeflies (below) are hoverflies that use their wicked-looking beak to suck nectar.

Hoverflies

Damselflies and dragonflies are fierce predators.

Small flies prey on even smaller ones

Damselflies rest with their wings alongside their bodies, but dragonflies spread their wings out.

FLY FACTS:

There are over 60,000 species of flies in the world.
No true flies can eat anything except liquid food.

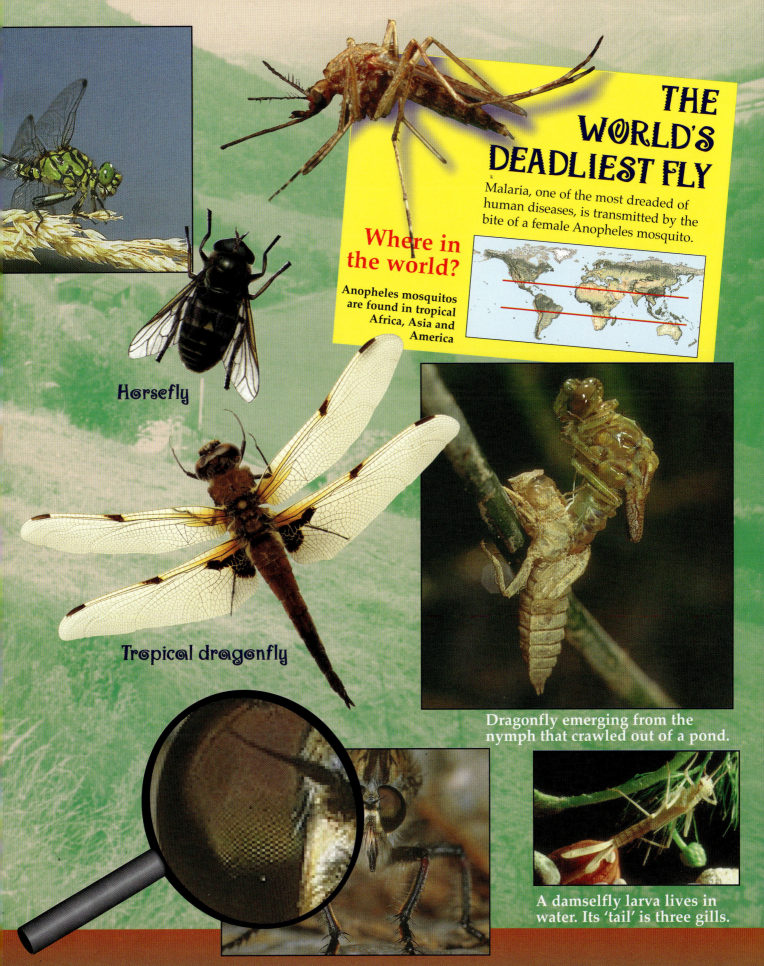

THE WORLD'S DEADLIEST FLY

Malaria, one of the most dreaded of human diseases, is transmitted by the bite of a female Anopheles mosquito.

Where in the world?

Anopheles mosquitos are found in tropical Africa, Asia and America

Horsefly

Tropical dragonfly

Dragonfly emerging from the nymph that crawled out of a pond.

A damselfly larva lives in water. Its 'tail' is three gills.

A close up of a robber-fly's eye.

BEES & WASPS

Common Wasp

Bees and wasps (plus their close relatives the ants) are among the most amazing insects in the world. Although many species, like the halictus bee (right), live alone, others live in huge, highly-organised societies.

Bee and wasp society revolves around one or more queens, fertile females that spend their entire life laying eggs. The other members of the colony care for the larvae, hunt for food, and build, repair and defend the nest. All these workers are females. The only job for males is fertilising the new queens, just once in a lifetime.

Wasps feed their larvae on fresh meat. Later in the year, adults go hunting for sweet food to help them to stay alive as long as possible. Bees feed their larvae on nectar and pollen. Wasps use wood chewed into paper to make their home; bees make theirs from wax.

Another difference between bees and wasps is the sting, which is straight and smooth in a wasp but barbed in a bee. Wasps can survive after using their sting, but a bee's sting cannot be withdrawn so the bee loses a part of its body and dies.

Halictus Bee

Honeybee

Bumblebee

While this honeybee probes a flower for nectar, the hairy 'pollen baskets' on its back legs are already packed.

BEE FACTS:

A honeybee colony can contain up to 80,000 workers. The Greeks knew that honey helps to heal wounds but science has only recently shown that this is true.

ADVANCE OF KILLER BEES

In 1956, the Brazilian government tried to cross some bad-tempered but very productive bees from China with some ordinary honeybees. The aggressive cross-bred bees escaped, and have been moving north for 40 years. They have now reached Arizona and California.

Where in the world?
'African killer bees' came from China, went to Brazil, and are now in California.

Paper wasps

Two wasp species on one pear.

Hornet

Buff-tailed bumblebee

Honeybee

Close-up of a spider-hunting wasp attacking a spider.

GRASSHOPPERS & CRICKETS

Together with roaches, stick insects and mantises, grasshoppers and crickets make up a very ancient group of insects. Mainly vegetarian, with a powerful pair of jaws for slicing through leaves, many species are hard to spot even though they may be large.

Unusually for insects, grasshoppers and crickets are very noisy. The males make their mating song by rubbing a rough part of their thigh against a wing-case. Their ears are on their legs, too! But being noisy doesn't make them any easier to find, because it is very hard to tell which direction the sound is coming from!

Their babies hatch as tiny wingless versions of the adults. At each moult, as the baby grows bigger, the wings also grow bigger until they are finally full-sized and the baby has become an adult. When the weather is warm enough, grasshoppers and some crickets can spread enormous wings and fly away to find new feeding and breeding grounds.

Stick insects are harder to see than grasshoppers. They are not great travellers, and do not make a noise. The males of some species have never been seen, and nobody knows if males even exist!

This little hopper has a long way to grow. Each time it moults, its wings will become longer until they are fully formed.

Green bush-cricket

GRASSHOPPER FACTS:
Some grasshoppers can jump the human equivalent of the length of two football pitches.

This stick-insect seems to have peeling bark and long, flat leaves.

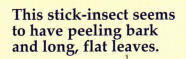

A BIBLICAL PLAGUE

A swarm of locusts on the move can strip every green leaf for hundreds of miles. The largest swarm of locusts ever recorded was supposed to be 2,000 miles wide as it crossed the Red Sea around 100 years ago.

Where in the world?

Locust swarms can occur on every main continent of the world.

A thorny Asian stick insect

Grasshoppers are divided into two main groups: long-horned ones like this and short-horned ones like locusts.

A newly-hatched hopper's colour gives it away as it poses on a rose.

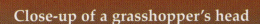

Close-up of a grasshopper's head

MOTHS

There are many more species of moths than butterflies, and their caterpillars eat a wider variety of foods. As well as leaf-eaters, there are wood-borers, fruit-eaters, wax-eaters, fur-eaters and feather-eaters.

Some fur-eating moths live happily among the woollies in our homes. Some that live inside fruit are known as orchard pests. But we rarely notice many others.

Moths need to use senses other than sight for finding food and mates. One of a moth's important senses is its sense of smell, which is located in its antennae. Flowers have scent to attract moths. Some moths have such a brilliant sense of smell that a male can find a female miles away, just by following the scent trail in the air! The antennae of some larger moths are feathery in males and plain in females.

Not all moths are interested in light, but the ones that bang on our windows or fly around lamps are really trying to go in a straight line. For millions of years the only lamp they had was the moon, and because it is so far away they could use it to fly a straight course. You could do the same. But if you chose a streetlamp, you would go round in circles too!

The Imperial silkmoth (left) is one of the species bred for silk.

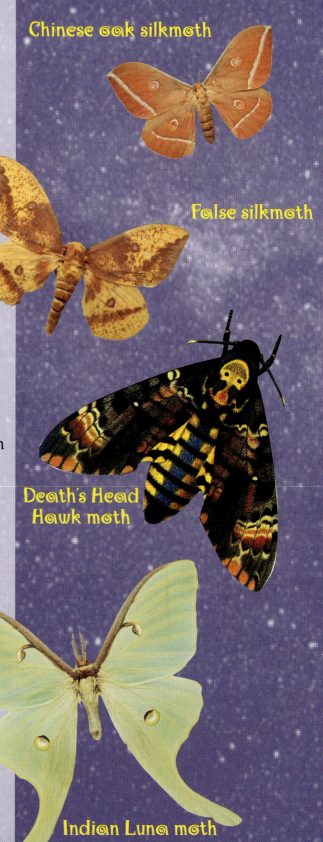

Chinese oak silkmoth

False silkmoth

Death's Head Hawk moth

Indian Luna moth

MOTH FACTS:

A male Emperor moth can smell a female more than 6 miles away.
20,000 moth species are less than 1/4 inch wide.